SHAPES = MGA HUGIS

Learn tagalog in English

SHAPES IN TAGALOG FOR KIDS

PICTURE BOOK

AMIHAN BALASABAS

Circle
bilog

Arrow

palaso

Triangle
tatsulok

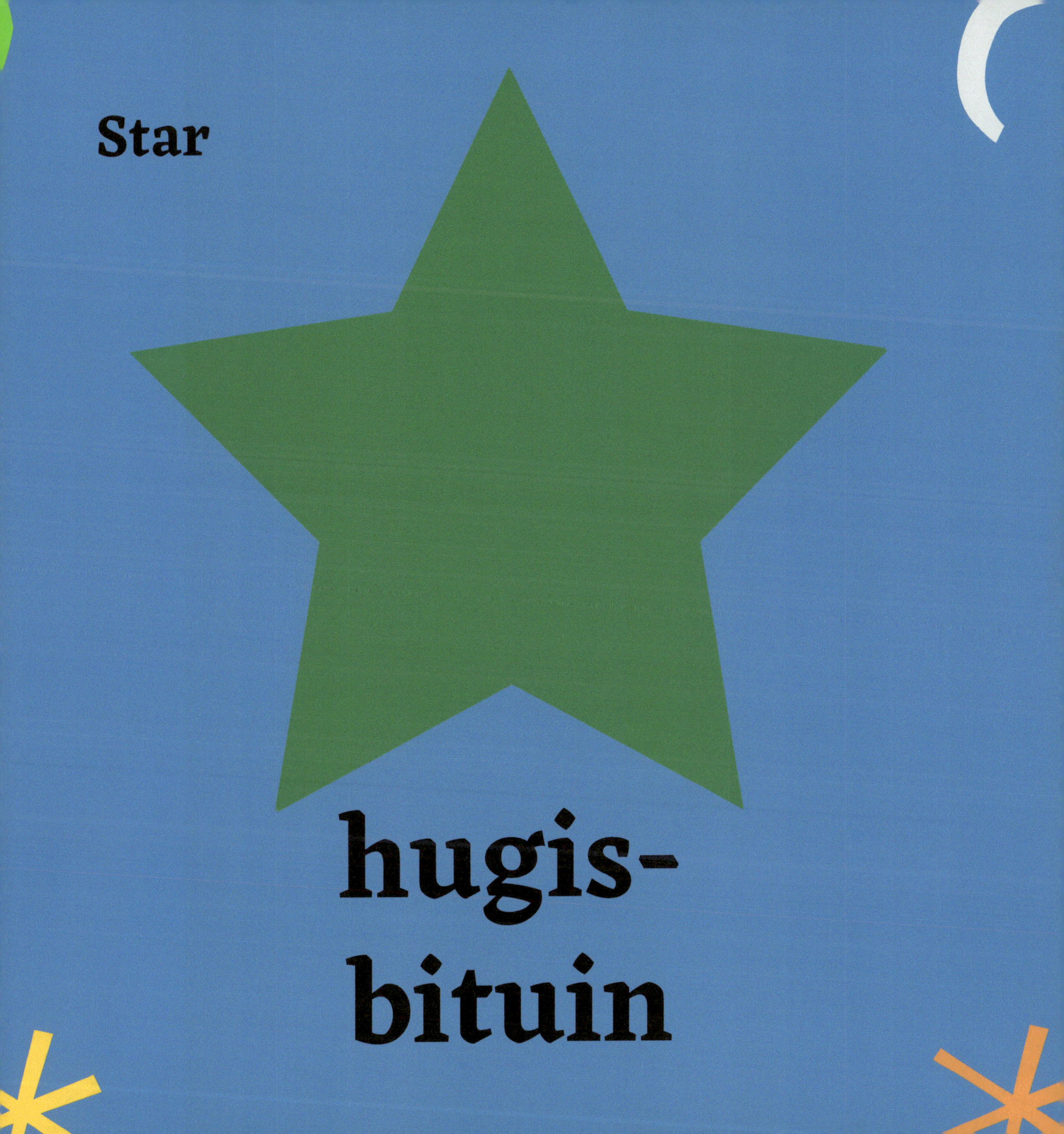# Star

hugis-
bituin

Semi Circle

kalahati ng bilog

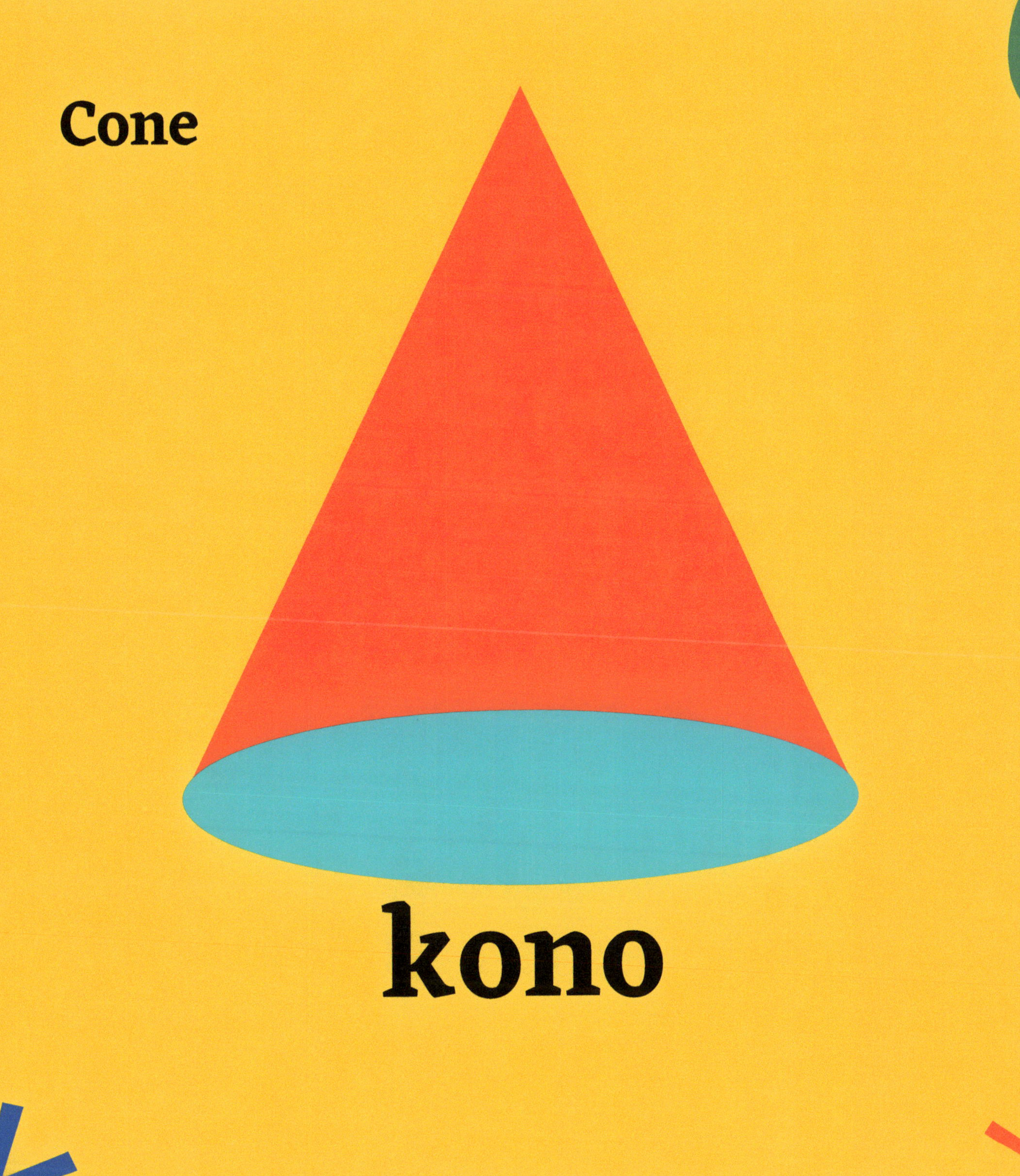
Cone
kono

Square

parisukat

Hexagon

eksagono

hugis-puso

Oval
habilog

Cube

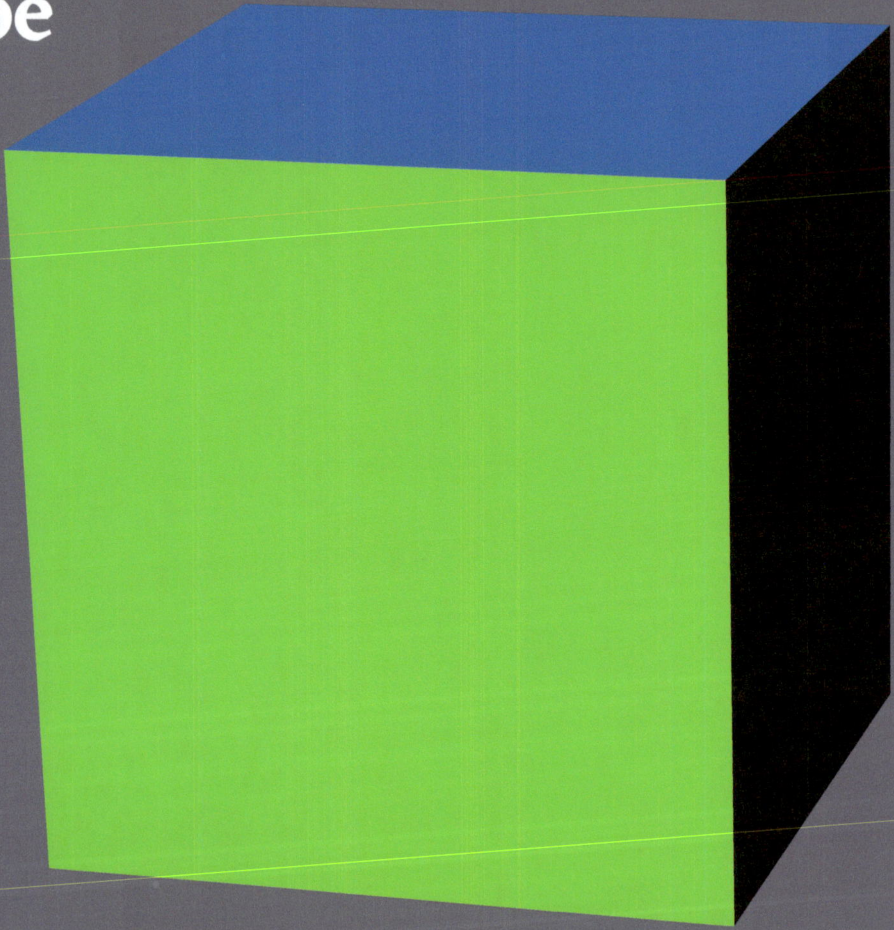

kubo

Diamond

hugis-diamante

Parallelogram

parigapay

Trapezium

tagigapay

pentagono, limsiha

Pyramid

piramide

Spherical
globo, espera

Decagon

pulsiha

hugis-krus

Rectangle

parihaba

Crescent

gasuklay

Cylinder

silinder

Plus

aumento

pagbabawas

Division

paghahati

pagpaparami

katumbas

oktagono

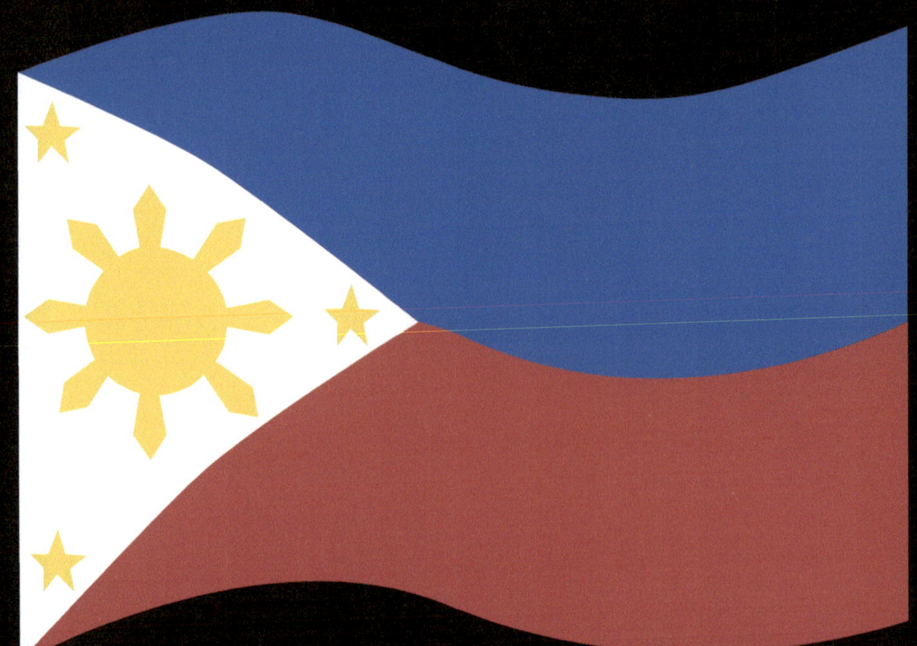

I hope you liked this book. Please check out my other books. Thank you.

https://www.amazon.com/Amihan-Balasabas/e/B092G79MMM

sa muling pagkikita

salamat

Amihan Balasabas